MONEY SEEDS

30 FINANCIAL PRINCIPLES

Lawrence Cain, Jr.

Copyright © 2017 Abundance University

All Rights Reserved.

This book may not be reproduced, transmitted, or stored in whole or in part by any means, including graphic, electronic, or mechanical without the express written consent of the publisher except in the case of brief quotations embodied in critical articles and reviews. Abundance University, 2017

Money Seeds: 30 Financial Principles

Table Of Contents

A MESSAGE FROM THE AUTHOR — Pg. 6

PRINCIPLE #1: **Pride doesn't pay bills, productivity does.** — Pg. 9

PRINCIPLE #2: **Don't go after 'job security'; build income security.** — Pg. 10

PRINCIPLE #3: **Under pressure it's normal to sweat, not get into debt.** — Pg. 11

PRINCIPLE #4: **Financial success happens on purpose.** — Pg. 12

PRINCIPLE #5: **We don't have an income problem; we have a priority problem.** — Pg. 13

PRINCIPLE #6: **If cash is king, credit is the ace.** — Pg. 14

PRINCIPLE #7: **Retail therapy never works.** — Pg. 15

PRINCIPLE #8: **Even millionaires have budgets; theirs are just bigger than ours.** — Pg. 16

PRINCIPLE #9: **Relationships can carry you further than a resume.** — Pg. 17

PRINCIPLE #10: **Manage your bank accounts like you manage your social media accounts.** — Pg. 18

PRINCIPLE #11: **The goal is to be good, not just look good.** — Pg. 19

PRINCIPLE #12: **You have everything you need to get everything you want.** Pg. 20

PRINCIPLE #13: **Judge each day not by its harvest, but by the seeds you sow into it.** Pg. 21

PRINCIPLE #14: **Investing has more to do with discipline than it does the amount you invest.** Pg. 22

PRINCIPLE #15: **Control your spending by controlling your emotions.** Pg. 23

PRINCIPLE #16: **Financial talks can cure financial struggles.** Pg. 24

PRINCIPLE #17: **Teach your kid(s) how to be a producer and not just a consumer.** Pg. 26

PRINCIPLE #18: **Remember the seed is always smaller than the harvest.** Pg. 27

PRINCIPLE #19: **What you buy shows how much money you had, not how much money you have.** Pg. 28

PRINCIPLE #20: **Owing businesses that don't invest back into your community isn't acceptable anymore.** Pg. 29

PRINCIPLE #21: **Cash flow is the secret to financial freedom.** Pg. 30

PRINCIPLE #22: **We don't get paid for time or seniority; we get paid for value.** Pg. 31

PRINCIPLE #23: **Your behaviors should match your beliefs.** Pg. 32

PRINCIPLE #24: **Collaboration is better than competition.** Pg. 33

PRINCIPLE #25: **Money looks better in the bank than on your feet.** Pg. 34

PRINCIPLE #26: **Some people buy fish, others buy lakes.** Pg. 35

PRINCIPLE #27: **Insurance: It's better to have it and not need it, than to need it and not have it.** Pg. 36

PRINCIPLE #28: **Time is not money. Time is more valuable than money.** Pg. 38

PRINCIPLE #29: **Focus on income producing activity.** Pg. 39

PRINCIPLE #30: **Some people want $50K a year, some people want $50K a month.** Pg. 40

RESOURCES Pg. 41

ABOUT THE AUTHOR Pg. 47

A MESSAGE FROM THE AUTHOR

Back in 2010, the regional director of career services of my college walked up to me and asked, "Hey Lawrence, what are your plans after graduation?" It was my last quarter of school, and I really hadn't thought about this (like most people in college). My response was simple to say the least. "Getting a good job," I replied. With the most serious face I've ever seen, he stated "That's all good, but what will you be doing at that job? Once you figure that out, you'll be set for life." After that conversation, I searched deep inside myself to figure out what it was I wanted to do. The answer came sooner than I thought.

While doing some homework for my Personal Finance class, I found myself looking up words from the glossary even after I finished my homework. The light bulb went off in my head. "I want to work for a bank," I said to myself. I didn't grow up around anyone who could teach me about money, so I figured working around money while at the same time learning financial lessons was the best idea. From there, I applied at three banks, interviewed at two, and accepted a position at one. For the past 7 years, I've been in the financial world. It has been a lot of ups and downs, but all of my experiences have led me to start my own company as well as write this book. The late great Zig Ziglar once said, "Money isn't everything, but it ranks up there with oxygen." How true that quote is even in today's society.

    This workbook is meant to give you clarity, wisdom, and empowerment for your financial journey. There are 30 principles with questions following each principle. The questions are intended to make you dig deep like I did back when I was in college. Without understanding what you're after, you'll probably always feel like the donkey chasing the carrot. Financial success happens on purpose, so use this book to get closer to all of your financial goals!

Principle #1: Pride doesn't pay bills, productivity does.

Many people in America struggle; not because the inability to perform job duties, but because they let their ego stop them from doing what they have to do to get ahead financially. They say things like "They don't pay me enough to do that" and "They couldn't pay me to do that type of job." That way of thinking stops people from actually getting to their goals. A second job that pays less doesn't mean you're less of a person; it means you're aware that you need more money faster to pay off debt, save for kid's college, etc. Make sure you exercise ALL options when dealing with your financial goals. Some decisions will cause you to go against what you really want to do, but it will be worth it in the end.

Productivity is underrated and over needed. Pride hinders your goals and often times creates more work for you than need be. The beauty about being productive is that it creates good habits, and success is a bi-product of that. Have you ever said "there's not enough hours in a day"? That's usually a case of not being as productive as you really wanted. A tip for increasing productivity is writing down a schedule of your week on Sunday. If that's too much for you, just start with the next day and build from there. Bottom line is that your future success is linked directly to your current productivity, so live accordingly.

On a scale of 1-10, 10 being the most, where would you rank how productive you are financially and physically?

Principle #2: Don't go after 'job security', build income security.

Before I graduated college, I thought that job security was a real thing. Then I worked for one of the biggest banks in the nation; that's when I saw the light. One of the highest sales producer was fired for 'undisclosed reasons.' She made 5 times more sales than I did, and to see that she was there one day and gone the next caused me to think about what we are really after. At the end of the day, we are all after producing income for our efforts. So the new focus is income security, and making sure you build skills and relationships that will almost guarantee you income for your working years.

20 years ago, jobs valued employees and respected those who were loyal. Now, most jobs focus more on profit than on their people. If you work for a company that has high turnover, gives out mediocre raises, or never implements employee's ideas, it's safe to say there isn't any job or income security there. Income security comes from the set of skills, relationships, and ambition you possess. If you need to increase your skillset, develop new relationships, and create a better sense of urgency, YOU CAN DO IT!

Write down 2-3 skills that you either possess or would like to possess that can generate income.

_____

_____

Principle #3: Under pressure it's normal to sweat, it's not normal to get into debt.

    I know people that felt that they had to go to college because their family members pressured them to. Because of that, they are in debt and they don't even work in the field in which they went to school for. Other people I know are in terrible car payment situations, paying over $400 a month for a car that isn't even their dream car. Instead of taking their time and actually getting the best deal possible, they let the pressure of having their own car put them into a situation where they're giving up more money than necessary. One of the most important things a person needs in finance is patience. In a microwave society, we need to take a crockpot approach to our money matters.

    Pressure bursts pipes, but pressure also makes diamonds. We all will have trials and tribulations, but it's all about how we respond to them. Planning ahead really helps with those unexpected expenses. When making a budget, you should always look at the next month to determine those special expenses that you know will come up (birthdays, car maintenance, etc.). This also helps with knowing if you need to increase your income, and in most cases that's the only solution living in a capitalistic society. No matter how much we try to cut expenses, making more money is more realistic.

What are some major purchases that you see yourself having to buy in the next 6-12 months?

_____

_____

_____

Principle #4: Financial success happens on purpose.

It's easy to get into a financial bind without having to put any thought into it. Just like weight: it's usually easier to gain pounds than it is to lose them. Furthermore, it takes intentional eating and exercise to lose the weight. Your financial freedom works the same way. When you know what you're after, the action steps have to get you to the destination. Being purposeful with your actions, energy, and spending, financial success becomes easier.

Being debt free, buying your house, sending your child to college, those are all goals that require some intentional actions. Nobody gets to college by accident, and nobody achieves financial success by chance. I want you to not only choose success, but implement the proper actions into your daily routine.

Make the vision plain, then make the action steps realistic and with specific deadlines.

What does financial success look like and mean to you and your family?

_____

_____

Principle #5: We don't have an income problem, we have a priority problem.

I've never seen an empty shopping mall or restaurant on any given weekend, yet we as a nation are billions of dollars in consumer debt. I see so many people on social media spending money on things they don't actually need, knowing that they just called me about helping them with their finances. When I do consultations, one question that I ask is "What is your favorite store?" The reason why I ask that is because being committed to someone else's bank account will not fix ours.

When meeting with clients, most of them have a positive cash flow. Then when we look at their bank statements it shows multiple meaningless purchases. I can't stress prioritization enough. "I don't have time in the morning to eat breakfast so I just stop at _____." Does this sound familiar? By not making budgeting, investing, and getting debt free a priority, we spend years and money on things that puts us in a worse situation. Don't wait for the right time to prioritize, create the time now.

Why do you spend money and what goals will cause you to change how you spend?

_____

_____

_____

Principle #6: If cash is the king, credit is the ace.

Growing up, many of my relatives advised me not to get a credit card. They said they were "doing me a favor." I found out that this is not the best way to start adulthood since buying a house, investing in real estate, and getting a reliable car takes good credit. Paying cash is always the goal. However, we can't ignore that in America credit is used to determine more than just interest rates. Even employers check your credit. Cell phone companies check credit to determine how much of a down payment you'll make with them. Great credit gives you leverage when dealing with advancing financially. It's important that we get our credit in good standing not only for us, but for the next generation.

If you're a parent, the importance of getting your credit in great shape now is just as important as saving for college. Just imagine being 18 years old with perfect credit. Now, you can get a reliable car with a low interest rate. Then you can save more money each month to get either a rental property or a starter house. "Cool" parenting needs to go from buying kids what they want now, to putting them in position for financial success in the future. Yeah, having nice clothes and up-to-date technology is good, but having great credit and assets are better.

What can great credit do for your overall cash flow?

Principle #7: Retail therapy never works.

Some people love to feel good, and spending money gives them that feeling. Transfer that same feeling towards paying off a debt, and I will almost guarantee you it will feel better than any new outfit or shoes. After a year, most retail therapy purchases go unused. The reasons why people do retail therapy is usual not tied to their goals, it's tied to not being or working towards those goals. Controlling why we spend money can help us save money, and keep our homes from being filled with junk.

One of the financial challenges we face as Americans is big businesses. They are so influential in our finances that they spend billions of dollars advertising and marketing their products and services to us. It's so bad that you can google something on your phone, then that same item will be an ad on your Facebook newsfeed. Overcoming this challenge is simple, but takes a lot of discipline. First, make a decision to only buy needs for 60 days. Secondly, check your bank account every day even if you don't spend any money. Thirdly, set price points for every item you plan to purchase and vow to never pay full price for anything, unless it's supporting a small business or friend.

Instead of shopping, what can you spend your money on to help benefit your financial success?

Principle #8: Even millionaires have budgets, theirs are just bigger than ours.

People hate restrictions on their finances. That's normal. Budgeting feels like you're putting a cap on your finances. It's the total opposite. Creating a budget helps you determine if the income you bring in is sufficient for your lifestyle, or if you need to increase it. If you want to spend more money, either get debt free to free up money or simply make more money.

Multi-billion-dollar companies create forecasting budgets. They predict monthly earnings, expenses, and potential expenses they may come against based on their goals. Your personal finances are the same way. You have to look at monthly expenses, income, and possible expenses based on your lifestyle and network. Having a budget allows you to determine if you need to earn more money to compliment the expenses on your budget. Don't be afraid or ashamed to make a budget. It's a benefit, not a burden.

Will it benefit you more to increase your income or become debt free? How much is your debt balance?

_____

_____

_____

Principle #9: Relationships can carry you further than a resume.

    Your resume shows employers what type of work you've done and who you did it for. Relationships show the type of person you are. When looking at furthering your career or business, look at your relationships. Who can you call that can help elevate you? Who do THEY know? These questions will serve as a barometer for the quality of your friends. If you don't have good relationships, you can always develop them. Go meet new people, volunteer at events, go back to your alma mater. There's nothing stopping you from growing connections that can one day turn into contracts or a big career move.

    Almost every week on my Facebook newsfeed, I see someone post "Who's hiring?" or "My job is hiring." Career Builder and Indeed are good for getting interviews, but there's nothing like getting a stamp of approval from somebody that's already working at the job you're applying for. I know this from personal experience. I've gotten people jobs at companies I was working at, and vice versa. Focus on building good relationships, expanding your network, and adding value to people and it will come back to you. Another thing you can do is document your accomplishments in your current position so that when people talk about you to potential employers, they can convey your value.

Who are 3 people in your network that can help you get to the next level financially or professionally?

_____

_____

_____

Principle #10: Manage your bank accounts like you manage your social media accounts.

Some people don't check their bank account every day, but will be on social media every other hour. Have you ever unlocked your phone to go to a specific app and by nature tapped the Facebook app? I know I've done it a few times. It's normal to go to social media throughout the day, and so should checking your bank accounts. Even if you didn't swipe your card or pay a bill, identity theft can still occur.

When adding new tasks to your day such as checking your bank account, don't feel like you have to rely on yourself. Set a reminder on your phone. Make sure you have your bank's mobile app. If you are unhappy with the balance, do something to increase it.

How many times per week do you check your bank account? Social Media?

Principle #11: The goal is to be good, not just look good.

Being debt free, owning your own house, paying bills on time, having your money making money…… these are more important than showing off liabilities. The clothes, the furniture, the cell phones, they don't add value to your life. Owning these items don't mean that you have any more money than the person without these "things." Far too often we place success on things that don't equate to real success. Understand that bills don't get paid by looks, unless you're a model.

If you achieve your financial and professional goals, everything you want will be accessible without compromising your sanity. Companies charge interest on furniture, appliances, and even pets! There is nothing wrong with shopping, having nice things, and living good. That's normal in today's society and you deserve to do those thigs. What I am suggesting to you is to make sure you are taking care of your financial responsibilities before you start focusing on lifestyle facade.

Is your finances where you want them to be? What purchases will you avoid next month that derailed you from your goals this month?

_____

_____

_____

Principle #12: You have everything you need to get everything you want.

When you're analyzing the resources you have to reach your goals, you'll find out what you need is already in your possession. It might be a person you haven't talked to in months that can get you to the actual person you need to talk to for a new job. Maybe it's one of your friends on social media that may be your business partner and you just need to share your vision with them. As crazy as it may sound, it might be YOU that's in your way. Are you procrastinating on updating your resume, making that call, going back to school, taking that test? Write down what you want, and the resources you already have.

When I first started my business, it was all about putting on financial empowerment seminars. I didn't own a space to host them. I didn't have a curriculum. I didn't have a following. I didn't have capital. However, I did have a relationship with my alma mater to be able to host the seminars for free. I did have notes and experiences from my past to create a valuable presentation with handouts. I did have social media and a phone with contacts in them to help me promote my event. I did have a job that I could work overtime for in order to generate extra money to invest in my company. Bottom line, start where you are, with what you have.

What are 3 goals you want to achieve in the next year? What resources do you have right now to get you there?

_____

_____

_____

_____

Principle #13: Judge each day not by its harvest, but by the seeds you sow into it.

When asked "How was your day", 9 times out of 10 people think of what happened to them that day and come up with their answer. Being late to work, forgetting your lunch on the counter, and having an argument with your spouse can make your day bad. On the other hand, getting a raise and reconnecting with a loved one can make your day great. Now when it comes to financial goals, we want to focus on what we actually did in our day that was a step towards our goals. Today, did you stay on budget, read for 30 minutes, work on that business plan, check your bank account, etc.? Those are just examples of seeds you can sow, but you know what they are specifically for you. When people ask me what I've been up to, I simply say "Sowing seeds."

Just like achieving fitness goals, financial results don't show up overnight. It can take months to start seeing the fruits of your labor, so that's why focusing on the seeds and not the harvest is key. Also, understand that even when you get a piece of the harvest you still need to sow seeds. Yes, celebrate the promotion, the new job, the 'paid-in-full" letter from your student loan company. Just remember that you won't continue to get harvests if you don't continue to sow seeds.

What is the harvest you're striving for? What seeds can you sow daily to ensure the harvest?

_____

_____

Principle #14: Investing has more to do with discipline than it does the amount you invest.

A lot of people feel they have to wait until they make a certain amount of money to start investing. Enter the story of Theodore Johnson. Johnson worked for UPS for over 30 years, and never made more than $14,000 a YEAR! While working, he decided to treat investing like a tax, and invested every single time he got paid. Because of his discipline, he retired with a net worth of over $70,000,000! In 2017, we have so many stories about pro athletes going broke because they mismanaged their millions, so we have to believe that it takes discipline more than it takes a lot of money.

When you decide to invest, pick an amount that you won't miss. $25-$100 should be your starting point. From there, meet with 2-4 financial advisors to get their opinions on funds you should invest in based on your financial goals. Make them work for you and with you. Consider adding an extra $100 per month each year to really gain momentum on the compound interest. Investing, just like working out, is only hard when you don't know how and what to do. The more clarity you get, the more fun it will be doing it.

How much can you start investing per month right now that won't alter your current lifestyle?

_____

_____

_____

Principle #15: Control your spending by controlling your emotions.

Getting rid of your emotions towards money can help out you and the generations after you. Do we know people who are addicted to shopping? Addicted to a specific brand of coffee? It happens, and rightfully so. It feels good to spend money on things we love, and it feels bad to spend money on bills and unexpected expenses. By taking our emotions out of our finances, we see money for what it is, a tool to provide a certain lifestyle.

Looking at your goals every day can eliminate the emotional impulse buying. It will help with "retail therapy." If you lost $100 today, how would it affect your mood tomorrow? If the answer is negative, remember that you control how much money you make rather you spend it on bills or lose it.

How long does it take you to make a purchase?

Principle #16: Financial talks can cure financial struggles.

Too many relationships end over finances, and it's usually avoidable if the people would just sit down and talk it out. By talking, we can identify the challenge, convey our feelings about it, and work on a solution. Financial talks may be difficult, but very much needed. Remember, not all of us came from positive financial language backgrounds. That's why I caution you not to speak out of anger when it comes to the finances. No matter the relationship, it is important to keep constant communication whether good or bad.

     Proper communication can help bad financial situations turn around for the better. It's not fair to have one person in charge of EVERYTHING financially in the household, unless you both come up with that agreement. Even then, you still have to communicate about bills, goals, vacations, budgets, etc. You may be a person who doesn't understand finances as well as your spouse. You might be more financial literate than your spouse. Whatever your situation is, schedule time to review finances. Once every other month is sufficient enough, unless your family encounters a special situation that alters the financial flow (i.e. expecting a child, new promotion, laid off of current job).

When was the last time you talked to a loved one about your financial situation?

_____

Who controls the finances in your household?

_____

How often do you review your finances (budget, loan balances, and investment accounts)?

Principle #17: Teach your kid(s) how to be a producer; not just a consumer.

      To determine one's net worth, you subtract the liabilities from assets. Due to many factors, we've inherited mental liabilities and we contribute a lot of our spending power to other people's assets. We live in a dependent society where we pay for companies to provide services and products we can produce ourselves. Convenience is what we pay for. The drawback to this is that now kids are not being taught how to produce, but how to consume. Not just with electronics, but with food, gardening, household tasks, the list goes on. For the next generation, we have to teach and encourage them to produce the things that they consume.

      Many public schools do not offer Woodshop or Cooking: 101. Electives have gone to technology classes, which isn't a bad thing. Standardized testing teaches our kids how to prepare to answer questions about subjects that they may not even look at after high school. We have to go back to teaching how to create and not just how to dispose. Apprenticeships are also a good way to expose youth to skills that will provide income security. Before they leave the house they need to complete the Independent Checklist found in the Resource section of this workbook.

What's one product that you or your kid(s) use that you can research how they can make it themselves?

_____

Principle #18: Remember the seed is always smaller than the harvest.

Every type of seed on earth, from a tree to a fruit, is smaller than the harvest. While going through the week, it can be a challenge to stay on point with your financial goals. Family, job responsibilities, lack of sleep, these all are things that can throw you off track. That's why keeping a daily planner or utilizing you cell phone can assist you. Always keep your mindset on sowing seeds; the harvest, good or bad, will come from the seeds you sow and water.

You will also have to remember to water your seeds. If you started reading or writing a book, you'll need to dedicate time for finishing what you started. Continue to communicate with those individuals that can help you get to that desired harvest. Get proper sleep to make sure you have energy to be efficient with your time. Even when you achieve one of your goals, you still should focus on sowing seeds.

Write down your schedule for the next 2 days, from when you wake up till when you lay down for bed. Are there some seeds in your schedule? (Use your phone or a piece of paper)

Principle #19: What you buy shows how much money you had, not how much money you have.

Society and classism paints a false picture when it comes to materialistic ownership. Just because you see someone driving a foreign car or wearing the latest name brand clothes doesn't mean they have money. That means the money they HAD was spent on these items. Focus on buying assets, not liabilities. You can spend $175,000 on a house that you pay $1,200 a month, or you can spend $175,000 on a 4-family apartment building and get *paid* $1,200 a month (that's after you pay the mortgage by the way).

Be careful not to follow purchasing trends. A lot of Americans have spent money on trendy clothes just for them to go out of style the next year. Not only that, but as you grow older your taste in music, clothes, cars, or entertainment could possibly change. Your weight could change and cause you not to fit in clothes you paid top dollars for. That car you bought brand new off the lot decreases in value significantly after 3 years, while you still are making payments for 2-4 more years. Use your money to buy assets, and let the assets buy you the fun stuff.

What do you own that is making you money? What are some assets you want to acquire in the near future?

Principle #20: Owing businesses that don't invest back into your community isn't acceptable anymore.

    We must take back control over our finances, and we have to realize that who we choose to do business with says a lot about how we really care about our money. Supporting local businesses is the ideal decision, but they also need to earn our business. Nike, Disney, Apple, and Amazon all get billions of our dollars, yet they don't use that money to hire more of us nor do they invest into our communities. Make it a personal goal of yours to spend less with big businesses and do more business with friends, family, and businesses that are really for us.

    In 2016, Flint, Michigan had issues with their water supply that made national headlines. Tons of non-profit organizations, including one that I'm a board member on, came to the aide of the Flint residents and provided as much help as possible. Bottled water was donated by millions of Americans, but many companies that resided in Flint opted not to contribute. Also, the water company to this day is trying to sue residents for their corrupt mistake. Just like in the civil rights era, we have to hit these companies where it hurts, in their bank accounts.

What businesses do you support that support your city/community? What companies can you start supporting?

_____

_____

_____

Principle #21: Cash flow is the secret to financial freedom.

      Cash flow has two components: frequency and amount. You have to know how frequent money comes in, how frequent it goes out, and the amount of both flows. Positive cash flow is when you have more money coming in, than money going out. Negative cash flow is more money going out than coming in. Most of us get paid twice a month, but spend money every day. Make it a goal to get paid more frequently, and to spend less frequently.

How often do you get paid?

_____

How much is your monthly income?

_____

How much do you pay in actual bills each month?

_____

How much do you spend on leisure items?

_____

Is you cash flow positive or negative?

_____

Principle #22: We don't get paid for time or seniority; we get paid for value.

    The days in which we got paid for time and/or how long we've been at a job is over. In this information and technology-driven world we live in, we have to retrain our mind around how we get paid. The value we bring to any marketplace will determine how much money you'll make, not your salary. Entrepreneurship is becoming the new norm because people recognize companies aren't giving out raises as fast as the cost of living increases. If you want to make more money, you have to identify which marketplace you can add value to. From there, determine if that value is you changing careers, partnering with someone, or starting your own company.

Personally, I knew no company could pay me for the type of value I provide without me having to go back to school. That wasn't realistic for me. It may be for you, if your job offers tuition reimbursement. Understanding your true value will help you determine how to move professionally.

What are 3 things you can do/create that can increase your value in your desired field?

_____

_____

_____

Principle #23: Your behaviors should match your beliefs.

Don't tell people what you're trying to do financially if your behaviors don't match your beliefs. You can't say you're going to lose weight if you're eating poorly, just like you can't say you're getting your finances together if you're spending poorly. Positive financial behavior includes: planning in advance, creating a budget, saving money, paying bills on time, reading to increase value, etc. If you have trouble developing the belief, get around people who have both behaviors and beliefs that are in sync.

When I was 22 years old I started doing network marketing. No matter the company, I had the same goals. Coincidentally, I also had the same problem preventing me from making the money I thought I'd be making. My beliefs were big, but my behaviors we mediocre. I spent money on business cards, but never seemed to pass them out. I used to call 10 people a week instead of 10 people a day like we were trained to do. Once I realized that it was me getting in the way of my goals, I decided to focus on doing things that made sense for my goals. Fast forward 5 years and that's when I started my company Abundance University. My behaviors and beliefs can never be questioned by anyone, including myself.

Write down 1 behavior you wish to add to your lifestyle.

_____

Write down 1 behavior you'd like to change?

_____

Principle #24: Collaboration is better than competition.

Capitalism creates a natural competition factor. Companies compete for our business, people compete for job positions, and some people compete for status. One of the keys to financial freedom is investing, and for some that is a challenge. It doesn't take a lot of money to invest, as we saw with Theodore Johnson, it takes strategy. One of the oldest strategies in American investing is investment clubs. Just imagine getting a group of 9 people and all of you investing $25 a month for 40 years? How about $100 a month? What about $500 a month? This is something you should consider doing with trustworthy loved ones. It takes the pressure off of each individual to have to invest by themselves. We know there's strength in numbers, so use that to your financial advantage.

When starting my company, I always wrote down 'we' when I could have put 'I' there. I knew I that I would have partners, affiliates, and advocates for the brand, even though I didn't know how they were going to come into my life. A year after I started my company I started getting people to partner with me on my seminars and financial coaching services. I've connected with people who have networks in states that I've never visited. Working together will help you get to your goals and allow you to be a part of other's success.

Who are 3 people that you can partner with that can get you closer to your financial and personal goals?

_____

_____

_____

Principle #25: Money looks better in the bank than on your feet.

Jordans cost $200 retail, and Pumas can cost $30 retail. Both are nice shoes, but Jordans cost over 6 times as much as some Pumas. When shopping, the goal should be to buy a nice item paying the least amount possible. This is what we call setting price points for items that you're going to spend money on anyway. Always think about getting deals. Always think about paying the least amount possible, because these companies are for profit. That's not to say that you should settle for low quality items, it means don't get out of pocket by giving up more money out of your pocket.

It's so funny when we go to schools and show them that the price of a share of Nike costs over $100 less than a pair of Nike shoes. They see that they can own the company, let the company pay them dividends, and buy the company's shoes with the dividends. What brands are you attracted to? Go to marketwatch.com and look at their stock table. You'd be surprised at how cheap stocks are. Buying stock creates assets, buying shoes create liabilities.

How much did you spend on shoes in the past 3 months? Is it more than how much you saved in that same timeframe?

_____

_____

Principle #26: Some people buy fish, others buy lakes.

When you think of Disney, you think about their animated movies. What most people don't know is that Disney also owns another major company, ESPN! I said that to say this, focus on working to own assets instead of working to just own stuff. They say if you give a man a fish, he'll eat for a day. If you teach a man how to fish he'll eat for a lifetime. Most importantly, if you teach a man how to own a lake, he'll eat for generations.

Life is short. When you look at what our ancestors had to overcome to get us to this point, it's an understatement to say that we need to be more serious about leaving an inheritance to the next generation. Not just money, but morals, connections, instructions (creating a will), as well as assets. I can't tell you how many people sit down with me and never think about the next generation. We want them to have a better life by buying them things, instead of positioning them to build empires.

What is going to be the lake you leave behind for your family? Are you on track to have it?

_____

_____

_____

Principle #27: Insurance- It's better to have it and not need it, than to need it and not have it.

Nowadays, GoFundMe has taken place of life insurance. It is important to have life insurance and also be properly insured. We know that we don't know the place nor time that we will pass away. Life insurance protects your family from not only your funeral expenses, but any assets and debts you have. Quiet as it's kept, a lot of Americans that know the power of life insurance are getting bigger policies so that when they pass away, their family will inherit more money than they actually need. If you don't have life insurance outside of your job, I highly recommend that you get some.

After I got married in 2014, we got life insurance from a good friend. We felt a sigh of relief that the funeral expenses were going to be covered. Then, I met a man that talked about being underinsured. I decided to meet with him for a consultation. It was free and he has been in the insurance industry since he was 19 so I trusted his knowledge. After he went through his questionnaire with me, he showed me how much we needed to be fully insured. The number was more than 4 times as much as we currently had! What made it even more incredible is that by switching to his company, we were going to pay less! As of today, he's one of our business sponsors and a good friend of mine.

Add up your total debt, assets, and the average cost of a funeral ceremony. How much is that? Do you have that in insurance coverage?

Principle #28: Time is not money. Time is more valuable than money.

We grew up with the "Time is money" mindset. Some people even have the phrase tattooed on them! That phrase sounds good, but the truth is quite the opposite. If you lose $100 today, you can make $100 tomorrow. If you don't do anything productive with your time today (but you're reading this book so hypothetically speaking), you cannot get the time back tomorrow. It's gone forever. Time efficiency is vital to your finances. You can control what you do and how fast you do it; money will follow suit.

As you start to understand your value in your marketplace, you can then look at ways to make your time worth your wild. Figure out how you can increase your income by $20,000. Figure out how you can increase it without working double the amount of hours. Find out how you can create an additional stream of income that can match your current income.

How much is your time worth? How will you increase you income without working twice as hard?

Principle #29: Focus on income producing activity. (IPA)

Busyness doesn't always equate productivity. There's 24 hours in a day, and your activities during your day will provide the amount of money you work for. For many of us, we don't know what activities will produce income. Also, there are people who know what they can do to make more money, but instead they choose to do things that lead to nothing. Money works, even if you don't work. Your IPA may be learning a new skill, promoting your friend's business, or even volunteering at your local school with the intent on networking with potential clients. Whatever your activities are, just make sure you put them into your daily schedule and DO THEM!

Scheduling your day will help out in this area. Plan out your day the night before. Factor in the income producing activities. Factor in how long you want to be doing those activities. Be realistic about the time too; 3 hours of typing your book may not be doable if you work 10 hours a day and have other obligations. Also, set a reminder to write down your schedule. Eventually you'll get to the point where it will become a habit and you'll be an expert on time management, which will translate into great money management.

Write down 3 income-producing-activities that you can do at least 3 times a week

_____

_____

_____

Principle #30: Some people want $50K a year, some people want $50K a month.

With technology being a big part of our lives, it's important to use it to your advantage. Set a goal to make $50,000 a month, then look at ways to get you there. Is it writing a book, joining a network marketing company, or even starting your own company? Remember, money is a result of your actions and it's up to you to make your actions get you to your desired income level. Think of the person you'll be if you get to that level of income.

I remember when I was working a job making $9.00 an hour thinking to myself, "Man, if I was making $12.00 an hour I would be good." Then, I started making $12.00 and felt like I needed more. $50K a month is $600,000 a year. What if you only make half of that? $300,000 is still a great income to have. Far too often we aim low and still never get to our target. Shooting high and not hitting the target can still mean having a great life. If you're going to work 40+ hours a week, make sure you make the maximum amount possible, without compromising your sanity.

How much do you want to make per month in 2 years? Now multiply that number by 3. What is it now?

Resources

For financial coaching/counseling, credit repair, and youth workshops, contact Abundance University at http://www.abundanceuniversity.net

Apps that help with managing finances

- Clarity Money
- Personal Capital
- Level Money

Apps for investing

- Acorns
- Robinhood
- Stash

Apps for credit monitoring

- Credit Karma
- CreditWise
- Credit Sesame

Budgeting Tips

Be Realistic About Your Budget
If you've never made a budget before, you need to start by forecasting how much money you'll have coming in every month and how much you think you'll be spending. The more realistic you are about each of these numbers, the more likely you'll be to stick to your budget.

Align Your Budget With Your Goals And Values
Once you've completed your budget, study it and see if you're spending your money in alignment with your values and goals (short-term and long-term). If you are having difficulty adhering to your budget, you may be overspending on things that aren't really aligned with your goals.

Guess Low For Income
In your budget, be conservative, and guess low for income. If your income exceeds the amount you factored into your budget, all the better! But you don't want to be caught short because you were overly optimistic.

Guess High For Expenses
In addition to guessing low for income, guess high for expenses. This, too, will give you some wiggle room when something unexpected crops up or costs rise.

Include a Miscellaneous Category In Your Budget
Take all of your expenses and total them. Then, take 10% of that total and put it into a "miscellaneous" category. This adds even more flexibility to your budget, helping to ensure that if you've omitted something from your calculations, you won't go over budget.

Include Savings As An Expense In Your Budget
Decide on an amount you'd like to save each month, and include it as an "expense" in your budget. Set up a separate savings account and transfer or deposit money into it every month. Your savings can be used for short-term goals (vacation) or long-term goals (college tuition or a house). This money can also be used in case of an emergency (car repair or medical expense)

Keep All Of Your Bills and Receipts Organized
Organizing your bills and receipts as you go along also makes it simple to file your taxes at the end of the year. There are certain mobile apps that can help make this task easier.

Review And Recalculate Your Budget
Reviewing your budget every month can help you stay on track with your finances. In essence, a budget is a forecast of what will happen; take the time to go back and recount what actually did happen. Where did you overspend? Where did you save? What can you do differently next month? You'll also probably need to re-calculate your budget every 3 months, or whenever something changes dramatically in your financial life.

Investment Jargon

A lot of people choose not to invest their money not because they don't think it's the right thing to do, but because of the lack of understanding they have when it comes to the terms used in investing. The purpose of this sheet is to simplify these terms so that almost anybody can understand the meaning of them.

Goal of Investing: INCOME!!!

Capital Gains: The profit that comes from a stock, bond, or real estate

Index Funds: "Basket" or list of stocks that you invest in instead of picking them yourself

Asset Allocation: A system to divide your money into different types of investments using specific percentages that you set up in advance

Dollar-Cost Averaging: Keeping your asset allocation percentages consistent when your gains increase

Fiduciary: A registered investment advisor who gets paid for financial advice and, by law, must put the client's needs before their own

Fixed Income Annuity: A product offered by certain companies that guarantees a fixed income for life and a 100% guarantee on your deposits if there is any losses

Recommended Books To Read

Money: Master The Game by Tony Robbins
Power of Intention by Wayne Dyer
The Compound Effect by Darren Hardy
How to Budget Like a Boss by Emerald Sparks
Income Power by Jason Miles
7 Habits Of Highly Effective People by Stephen Covey
Always Know What To Say by Peter Murphy
As A Man Thinketh by James Allen
Debt-Free College, We Did It! by Lynn Lusby Pratt
The Brand Within by Daymond John
The 4-Hour Workweek by Tim Ferriss
Rich Dad Poor Dad by Robert Kiyosaki
Lower Your Taxes-Big Time by Sandy Botkin
9 Routines of Successful People by Jonas Stark
Leaders Eat Last by Simon Sinek
Now, Discover Your Strengths by Donald Clifton
Networking Is A Contact Sport by Joe Sweeney
How To Set Goals by Craig Ballantyne

Financial Independent Checklist

Often times in America, our young adults move out on their own prematurely; they really haven't laid down a proper financial foundation. This 'normal' practice has led to many financial hardships. Going forward, we would like this checklist to be learned and implemented across the country to ensure our young people maximize the time spent at home by completing this checklist.

Item #1: Save $5,000 on their own.

Item#2: Learn a skill or trade.

Item #3: Furnish their apartment before moving out.

Item #4: Start an investment account/investment club.

Item #5: Start building credit.

Most adults agree with me that by successfully completing these items before moving out will benefit generations to come. If you need help, feel free to contact Abundance University!

About The Author.

Lawrence Cain, Jr. was born and raised in Cincinnati, Ohio. He gravitated to the business world at an early age after experiencing working for his grandparents at their local deli. After graduating college with a degree in business management, Lawrence ventured off into the finance industry. He's held positions such as personal banker, financial aid administrator, and loan specialist. While working, he decided to start doing public speaking, which he then created his company Abundance University. The 1st event put on by the company was a financial empowerment seminar, educating adults on the basics of personal finance. As of today, Abundance University has reached hundreds of people through financial coaching, credit repair, and workshops. Lawrence attributes his creation of Abundance University to the bible verse John 10:10, that states "… I came so that they may have life, and have it more abundantly."